DIVINE
Inspirations

From My **SOUL** *To Yours*

TAWNYA DAWN

BALBOA
PRESS
A DIVISION OF HAY HOUSE

ISBN: 978-1-4525-5971-1(sc)
ISBN: 978-1-4525-5972-8(e)
ISBN: 978-1-4525-5973-5(hc)

Balboa Press books may be ordered through booksellers or by contacting:

Balboa Press
A Division of Hay House
1663 Liberty Drive
Bloomington, IN 47403
www.balboapress.com
1-(877) 407-4847

Library of Congress Control Number: 2012919906

Printed in the United States of America

Balboa Press rev. date: 10/15/2012

DEDICATION

For my mother, Jill Rosales, the brightest star in my Universe. You never gave up on me or stopped believing in my dream. You encouraged me to be vulnerable with my artistry and to take a risk and share it with the world. You have shown me how to shine even during the darkest moments of my life. You have taught me by example what it truly means to be a Warrior of the Light! Thank you for loving me as deeply as you do. I love you, all the way up to God, your Sweet Pea, Tana

ACKNOWLEDGEMENTS

First and foremost I would like to thank God, my Creator, for being my greatest source of strength, for without that connection, nothing would be possible. I want to thank my Aunt Judy for introducing me to my spiritual path as a little girl, although it took me many years to start my own practice, I will be forever grateful to you for planting that beautiful seed; I know you are shining down from Heaven and sharing your brilliance with me. I want to thank my Papi, Luis Rosales Shaw and my Tio Jorge Rosales Shaw for instilling in me at a young age the power of knowledge, it is how I got to be here today with my love of poetry and literature. I want to thank my grandmother, Olive Marguerite Wise and my abuelita, Ana Mercedes Shaw de Rosales for loving me whole-heartedly and for teaching how to be kind and compassionate; your love will forever remain in my spirit; it is through that love that I shine as bright as I do today. My son, Devon Angelo Rosales, you are the sunshine of my life, you always believed in me, you taught me how to live life to its fullest, the day you were born my life was altered, God knew exactly what I needed, I will be forever grateful to your soul for choosing to experience this journey with me. My wonderful husband Steve, who has been such a great provider and patriarch of this family, thank you for being my rock, I did it baby, I did it! To my brother bear, Larry Gastelum, thank you for being such a huge to support to not only myself but to my family, you are the brother I never had, I love you with all my heart, til the wheels fall off! To my anam-cara, Susana Veiga, your love and support over the past twenty one years has sustained me and my spirit more than you will ever know, through our friendship I have learned what it truly means to know loyalty, mutual respect, and unconditional love. Carol Morrison, my blue-eyed-soul-sister, your love and support and belief in me will transcend space and time, I know you are shining and smiling down on me from Heaven, the sunshine train has arrived.....choooo choooooo....all aboard.....I love you Carol! Yolanda Greer, I want to give a special thank you for giving me the book 'The Little Engine That Could', you mailed it to me at a time when I was losing "steam", and it reignited my fire to continue on with this dream, words could never describe the gratitude I have for you! To my fellow poets and artists who have been some of the loudest and most zealous cheerleaders in my camp: Jill Rosales, Peter C. Rogers, Church Stanley, Moe Love, Lia Smith, Jimmie Chase, Kenny Washington, your love of poetry, higher thinking, exchange of literature and emotional support has been amazing; I will be forever grateful to you! To all of my wonderful Facebook friends who have cheered me on and have given me such great feedback on the inspirations I was posting, I know it sounds silly, but it means more than words could ever describe! It has been a very long road, your love and support of my dream did not go un-noticed! I want to give a huge thank you to some of the greatest ancient philosophers, poets, and writers of all time: Rumi, Osho, Pablo Neruda, Buddha, Lao-Tzu, Paramahansa Yogananda, Aesop, Confucius, Plato, Aristotle, Marcus Tullius Cicero, Epictetus, Marcus Aurelius, Gandhi, Kahlil Gibran; your artistry inspired me to rise above my physical pain and find relief in my greatest strength, my Spirituality. I would also like to thank some of my favorite present-day authors and poets: Louise Hay, Peter C. Rogers, Don Miguel Ruiz, Natasha Munson, Bo Lozoff, Iyanla

Vanzant, Marianne Williamson, Deepak Chopra, Wayne Dyer, Oriah Mountain Dreamer, Thich Nhat Hanh, Paulo Coelho, Mark Nepo, John O'Donohue, His Holiness The Dalai Lama, Melody Beattie, M. Scott Peck. I have been an avid reader since the age of nine, it was my escape as a child; and today it is a healthy reprieve from the outside noise. It is my great pleasure to share my Soul with all of you. I hope you continue to shine in the sunlight of God's spirit no matter what life throws your way. Shine bright, brighter than the sun! We are here to let our inner soul-shine radiate in its own brilliance, make today count! Yes! Let's do this!!!!

FOREWORD

BY-JULIANNE "JILL" ROSALES

I am the proud mother of the author of this book, which is not only an inspirational work, but a testament to a brave, courageous woman, who, through her own pain, and despite it, began a journey, resulting in this beautiful compilation of her own personal thoughts, quotes, and poems. After two back surgeries within a seven year time period, she was frustrated at the results, so my daughter began looking for spiritual solutions. She came upon literature from some of the greatest ancient philosophers; drawing inspiration to cope with her physical and emotional condition, which in turn reignited her own creativity. In her search of enlightenment and higher learning, I witnessed an inner transformation, a divine shift which transcended her heart and mind. She began to share her thoughts and quotes on Facebook, offering encouragement and comfort to others. The response was so positive from these posts, that the seed of this book was born.

I will forever cherish the moments I sat next to her as she worked at the computer, and she would enthusiastically share a quote with me. It was heartwarming to watch her become vibrant with life again. Through my daughter's love of quotes, poetry and philosophy; a beautiful new strength and purpose emerged. I feel, in a way, that writing this book, saved her soul and gave her the strength to continue on, against all odds.

The two of us visited Deer Park Monastery in San Diego to hear the Zen Master, Buddhist Monk Thich Nhat Hanh. When he spoke, he shared a simple observation:

"No mud – No lotus" for his teaching on suffering. He explains: "Without mud, you cannot have a lotus flower. Without suffering, you have no ways in order to learn how to be understanding and compassionate. Happiness is the lotus flower, and the suffering is the mud. So the practice is how to make use of the suffering, make use of the mud, to create the flower, the happiness, and this is something possible."

This profound statement suddenly made clear the essence of understanding the true beauty of my daughter's transformation. Only through her suffering could she really grasp the true essence of life. Tawnya, in my eyes, you are the Lotus in the truest sense of its meaning. You have experienced The Mud and have within your reach, The Lotus Flower. You have known suffering and have emerged into the sunlight of the spirit, The Flower.

INTRODUCTION

This collection of thoughts, quotes, and poems actually started out as a journal, something I did not plan on sharing with anyone. Writing again and delving into my creative side, became my own personal healing. Through allowing myself to process life's trials, tribulations, good days, bad days, gut-wrenching moments, happy moments, serene moments, shining moments, silent moments; I was able to rise above whatever I was going through and see the Light of God within me. I am taking the risk of allowing you the reader, a peek into my soul; in hopes that you will share yours with others and find the freedom I found, in being authentically me. Namaste.

Sometimes I feel as though in my tears I could drown

but my unbreakable spirit knows they are cleansing

and doesn't allow them to break me down.

So I smile and shine as bright as I can

until I am able to walk in the sunlight of the spirit again

like the child of God that I am.

MY THOUGHTS FOR THE DAY

A true "soul to soul" connection happens

when a person enters your heart

and touches the highest point of happiness in you;

they penetrate the most vulnerable part in your spirit.

They "see you" and you are never.....ever.....the same.

MY THOUGHTS FOR THE DAY

I have a burning desire

to know your soul

not the surface you

not what you want others to see

or what you hope to be

but the authentic you....the real you.

MY THOUGHTS FOR THE DAY

Out of nowhere

you blew into my life

like a hurricane...

and swept me off of my feet

like a sweet summer breeze.

MY THOUGHTS FOR THE DAY

Step into your God-given greatness

continue pushing forward and shining bright

regardless of any outside circumstances.

Stay in the sunshine and keep on smiling!

MY THOUGHTS FOR THE DAY

Don't let anyone rob you of your serenity

don't let anyone have a stronghold on your spirit!

It's time to take back your power

and shine like nobody's business!

Stay in the sunshine in all that you do.

Remember we are all destined for greatness

but you have to go out there and get it

it will not be handed to you

do the footwork and watch as the fruits of your labor

blossom within you!

MY THOUGHTS FOR THE DAY

PAIN

Drowning in my tears

suffocating in the words

my mind wants to express

but cannot imagine ever saying

dying in this deafening silence

fading into the abyss....

full of fear of the unknown

the what if's are weighing heavy on my mind

will I ever fly again???

MY THOUGHTS FOR THE DAY

A true friend is someone

who laughs with you when you are happy

who cries with you when you are sad

who supports you in life

who does not sit back and judge

who loves you unconditionally without strings attached

who lifts your spirit when you are in your darkest moments

and who will help you shine your brightest

when you are ready to fly!

MY THOUGHTS FOR THE DAY

Our passions, desires, hopes, and dreams

can be renewed on a daily basis.

Make sure you have short and long term goals

do something every day to work towards attaining them

even if it's just a little work

sometimes it takes baby steps to get to the summit

just do not ever stop climbing!

I will see you at the mountain top!

Keep it moving.

Stay positive.

Keep shining.

Let's do this!

MY THOUGHTS FOR THE DAY

You may not be able

to touch the scars

that have been seared

on your heart.....

but you can see them

through your eyes

the windows to your soul.....

MY THOUGHTS FOR THE DAY

Walk into the sunlight of the spirit

it is waiting for you

claim the happiness you deserve

you were always destined for greatness!

IT IS YOUR TIME TO SHINE!

MY THOUGHTS FOR THE DAY

Carrying the secrets of old pains

is like a fresh wound in the heart

that continually aches....

it never truly heals until it is revealed

only then will it die in the light of exposure

only then will the chains that bind the soul....be broken!

MY THOUGHTS FOR THE DAY

In silence the soul finds its own path

and a clearer brighter Light...

let your inner silence illuminate

what needs to be revealed to you...

and have the courage to listen to its guidance.

MY THOUGHTS FOR THE DAY

I am blooming like an exotic flower

that you have never seen before...

and you will never come across again.

MY THOUGHTS FOR THE DAY

Nobody has the power

to validate your existence but you!

So take the reigns back

and step into your brilliance!

MY THOUGHTS FOR THE DAY

Let go

or be dragged

grow and change

or decay

stay in the darkness

or shine like the sun

I choose to shine

in the spirit of God's Light

for only Love can set me free.....

MY THOUGHTS FOR THE DAY

In order to arrive

we must follow the signs

God is always whispering to us

in one way or another

it's about getting still

and paying attention to our soul

it's a matter of hearing the message

that is being sent to you

and then doing the footwork to get there!

ENJOY THE RIDE AND SHINE BRIGHT!

MY THOUGHTS FOR THE DAY

Each one of us

has a fire in our hearts

for 'something'

it is our purpose in life to find it

and keep the desire burning bright!

MY THOUGHTS FOR THE DAY

Just like the earth in the dead of winter

believes the sun will shine again and bring new life

I believe in our love and friendship.....I warm to you.

MY THOUGHTS FOR THE DAY

A gentle response will go much farther

than the wrath that follows anger and rage.

MY THOUGHTS FOR THE DAY

Stronger is a heart

that has taken the risk to love

and been shattered

than a heart

that has never been

vulnerable enough

to open itself up

to the 'possibility of love'....

MY THOUGHTS FOR THE DAY

My heart

has been seared

with scars....

and yet I continue to love

with all of my heart and soul

it's the way I was born

it's the way God intended it.

MY THOUGHTS FOR THE DAY

In giving voice to what we feel

the darkest cry uttered with honesty

can arrive as the most beautiful melody ever heard....

MY THOUGHTS FOR THE DAY

True authenticity

and self-acceptance come when you no longer feel the need

to apologize for who you are....

MY THOUGHTS FOR THE DAY

Your word

does not mean much

until you live up to it....

MY THOUGHTS FOR THE DAY

When you have life-long patterns of behavior

that are so deeply ingrained in 'who you are'

they cannot just be washed off like a smudge of dirt.

Sometimes it takes years to alter the dysfunctional

and unhealthy ways of living and thinking.

With effort, compassion and a desire to heal

miracles are possible.....they are waiting for you!

MY THOUGHTS FOR THE DAY

When someone treats you unkind

it is based on their own history of pain

try not to personalize it

it really has nothing to do with you

although this does not mean

we have to put up with this treatment

we just need to remember

it has to do with them

and nothing to do with us.

Let go....let God.....keep it moving.

RISE UP AND CONTINUE TO SHINE!

MY THOUGHTS FOR THE DAY

Sometimes life breaks us open

so that God can put us back together

stronger....better......brighter!

Maybe.....just maybe there is a purpose

for the pain we are experiencing today.

We need to use the pain as fuel

to propel us into the Light

so we can shine bright....

BRIGHTER THAN THE SUN!

MY THOUGHTS FOR THE DAY

What I have learned about internal wounds
is that they leave scars our hearts....
in order to bring them healing and a sense of peace
you have to dive into the wound
you cannot go under it
over it
around it...
you have to dive head first
full speed ahead with faith
dig in the wound
scream
cry
feel the pain
with all of your heart and soul...
and then fill the wound with love and truth
all these years I never know how much pain
I was still carrying in my heart and soul...
I am ready to expose my wounds and heal them
so I can truly shine in the sunlight of the Spirit
the way it was intended!

WALK WITH ME....FLY WITH ME......SHINE WITH ME!

MY THOUGHTS FOR THE DAY

I am not defined

by the mistakes I have made

I am not defined

by my accomplishments.....

I am defined

by the essence

of my shining spirit

and the way in which

I share it.....

MY THOUGHTS FOR THE DAY

Angry and resentful feelings will enslave us

but love, forgiveness and compassion

removes the chains that bind our soul to the darkness

and it frees us like nothing else ever could!

Stay in the Light......stay in Love.......

MY THOUGHTS FOR THE DAY

Happiness is a like a sunbeam

when it strikes a kindred heart

like lights upon a mirror...

it reflects with magnified brilliance

but it cannot reach its full potential

until it is shared!

MY THOUGHTS FOR THE DAY

People will try to rain on your parade

because they do not understand your sunshine

and they are so tired of their own darkness

instead of getting angry and frustrated with them

show them how to shine with love and kindness!

MY THOUGHTS FOR THE DAY

I still cannot believe you are not here

I measure the space you used to occupy

and fill with so much happiness...

large areas of my heart and soul

have now become vast and endless deserts

I cannot replace it with anything else

but the memory of you.....

MY THOUGHTS FOR THE DAY

A heart is a fragile thing

that is why we protect them so vigorously

why we give them away so rarely

and why it means so much

when we do and the love and respect

is reciprocated.

MY THOUGHTS FOR THE DAY

After all the pain

the struggles with daily life and its challenges

I guess the questions is:

how do we handle the journey into the heart of God?

My goal.....just for today

is staying on the path of love and enlightenment

that is where I will find the 'Heart of God'.

MY THOUGHTS FOR THE DAY

The warrior of the light finds her strength in pain

she knows she is stronger than her weakest moment!

She doesn't allow her pain to 'break her'

instead she uses it as fuel to propel her forward

to greatness and the ability to shine

in the sunlight of God's spirit....

MY THOUGHTS FOR THE DAY

Make your words sweet and warm like sunshine

they will penetrate the other person's heart more easily

they will hear you....and only love will be exchanged.

MY THOUGHTS FOR THE DAY

When we truly let go of the past

and the trials and tribulations

we have been through

we practice forgiveness and total acceptance

we give up the hope that the past

could have been any different

and in doing this

we need to mourn the past

accept it for what it was and move on

then we can shine bright.....brighter than the sun!

MY THOUGHTS FOR THE DAY

When I surrender to God's whispers

only then am I able to sparkle

in the sunlight of His Spirit.....

MY THOUGHTS FOR THE DAY

Other people's perceptions and opinions of me

does not define who I am

but how I choose to internalize them can.

No one can make me feel less than without my consent!

MY THOUGHTS FOR THE DAY

What goes up

must come down

what goes out

comes back around

watch yourself

keep your energy positive

and that's what you will get back!

Try it....you might like it.

IT'S TIME TO SHINE!

MY THOUGHTS FOR THE DAY

LIFE

FACE IT

EMBRACE IT

FEEL IT

HEAL IT

MY THOUGHTS FOR THE DAY

When you don't feel worthy of yourself

it is a direct insult to your creator.

Rise up.....dust yourself off

you were born to shine.....so act like it!

A warrior falls six times but stands seven!

Let's do this!

Walk with me

Fly with me

SHINE WITH ME....IT'S TIME TO RISE!!!

MY THOUGHTS FOR THE DAY

I never want to get stuck

on yesterday's enlightenment

I want to look at things with fresh eyes....

stay open minded

and keep my desire to shine bright

strong and vibrant

MY THOUGHTS FOR THE DAY

We need to stop sleep walking through life

God whispers to us through our intuition

then He nudges....the nudges start getting more and more clear

if we do not listen to the subtle messages life is sending

eventually we will be slam dunked into submission

we need to learn the lessons....grow......change

we are all destined for greatness

it's time to start acting like it

Let's all shine in the Spirit of God's Light today!

MY THOUGHTS FOR THE DAY

When you know better

and choose to do better

you get the opportunity

to rise to the best part

of yourself!

MY THOUGHTS FOR THE DAY

I no longer give people power over my emotions

people cannot hurt me

they are just sharing their perspective and opinion with me

it is up to me to choose what I do with it

I am the one that gives it meaning

this huge realization has been one of self-empowerment

MY THOUGHTS FOR THE DAY

You cannot make yourself

feel something you don't....

and you cannot pretend

you don't feel something that you do....

MY THOUGHTS FOR THE DAY

Roses do not bloom over night

beauty from within

takes time, sunshine, and nourishment.....

MY THOUGHTS FOR THE DAY

Energy cannot be destroyed

it can only be transformed

the energy we send out into the Universe

is like a boomerang

it always comes back to the source....

so keep your energy positive

and that's what you will get back!

MY THOUGHTS FOR THE DAY

The open heart

blooms like a flower

with her Beloved.....

MY THOUGHTS FOR THE DAY

There are a thousand ways

to embody your sunshine.....

find one that makes your heart smile

and bask in the brilliance of Love.....

MY THOUGHTS FOR THE DAY

There are times in life

when you will feel confused about everything

when you can't seem to figure out what your life path is

this is when you may have to change the direction of your journey

and go down the road less traveled...

you will know when you have arrived

it will feel uncomfortable because you are in unchartered territory

but trust and believe the Universe

will guide you back to your Soul....

MY THOUGHTS FOR THE DAY

Let's rise beyond all joy and sorrow

let's just 'be' in the moment

without judgement of feeling good or bad

let's practice being mindful of the air in our lungs.

MY THOUGHTS FOR THE DAY

I am the fragrance

of the most exotic flower

blooming for the first time

in spring......

MY THOUGHTS FOR THE DAY

For those of us who have been

to the depths of hell and back

dusted ourselves off and rose again

we will always continue to shine

we were not built to break

we are destined for greatness

WE ARE WARRIORS!

MY THOUGHTS FOR THE DAY

I will practice spiritual principles

even when no one is looking....

I will focus on my spiritual integrity.

MY THOUGHTS FOR THE DAY

Happiness cannot be acquired

happiness rises from the very depths of our souls

let your happiness rise today in all that you do!

MY THOUGHTS FOR THE DAY

Our only real job in life

is to recognize the Light within

and find what makes it shine the brightest

then share it with the rest of the world

it is not meant to stay closed up inside

and kept for ourselves

it is meant to be multiplied

in all its magnificence

it is God-given and can never be diminished

so bask in the sunlight of the Spirit

and show the world your SOUL-SHINE!

MY THOUGHTS FOR THE DAY

I saw God in the sunset this evening

it was absolutely breathtaking

it was pink....like the color of His happiness

dancing in the sky for all of us to marvel at

God's masterpieces are all around us

take some time to appreciate it and breathe it in....

MY THOUGHTS FOR THE DAY

Everyone needs a sacred space

that belongs to no one else but you

whether it be writing, reading, meditating,

painting, creating music......

whatever it is....it is all yours

and no one else's

it is your private reprieve into Self.....

MY THOUGHTS FOR THE DAY

As humans all we want from others

is to be truly seen, heard, and appreciated for who we are

to be told, "I hear you...I see you...you matter to me...I love you....."

MY THOUGHTS FOR THE DAY

Don't waste your energy

trying to change another's behavior

or their perceptions about life.

You will get frustrated

they will become defensive

and no one wins.

It is all about acceptance without expectations

that is true freedom in a relationship.

MY THOUGHTS FOR THE DAY

Whether it be a battle

of fists or one of words

no one ever wins....

however

self-restraint

self-love

self-esteem

always leads you down a victorious path...

MY THOUGHTS FOR THE DAY

Our need to win in the future

drains us of our power in the now!

Be mindful of the present moment

and the past and future

become unimportant factors

in your own happiness!

MY THOUGHTS FOR THE DAY

Too many of us at some point in our lives

have given somebody else control of our happiness

it is a hard lesson to learn especially when raised

in dysfunctional, co-dependent households

but once you learn that you hold the key to your own happiness

and you break the unhealthy patterns of learned behavior

then and only then will you truly shine

in the sunlight of the Spirit!

Happiness is an inside job....

start digging and find your own SHINE.....it's God given!!!!!

MY THOUGHTS FOR THE DAY

How does Mother Earth

share her smiles

and laughter with us?

Through flowers blooming

the sun shining

the moon's glow

the sound of the ocean

the majestic beauty of the mountains

the feel of a warm summer breeze on your face

the magic of seeing hawks fly above you.....

let it all in......and just breathe

these are gifts from the Creator

from God....from the Universe

being mindful of this very moment

all I feel is peace and serenity.....

MY THOUGHTS FOR THE DAY

Come here.....

come lay your hand on my heart

feel the way it beats

come read me sweet poetry

until I fall asleep

Come here.....

MY THOUGHTS FOR THE DAY

Your spiritual treasure

lies within your own soul

it contains everything

you will ever need

in this lifetime.....

MY THOUGHTS FOR THE DAY

Listening to music

is like breathing for me

the melody in music

is like air to my lungs

both are needed to exist.....

MY THOUGHTS FOR THE DAY

Let us not store up on

worldly collections

instead increase your

spiritual treasures

and watch as your spirit

starts to shine

in its natural state of brilliance.....

MY THOUGHTS FOR THE DAY

It's up to you whether you will allow yourself

to spend all your energy on what goes through your mind

you do not have to be the victim of your own emotions

not everything you think is based on reality

don't let your perceptions and opinions of 'self' break you

rise up and get God-centered

there you will find all the strength you need to shine!

MY THOUGHTS FOR THE DAY

Don't share your hopes, dreams, passions,

or desires with the world...

whisper them to God, to Love, to your own body, mind and spirit;

and watch as they bloom in the Spirit of Humility....

MY THOUGHTS FOR THE DAY

When somebody does or says something

negative or hurtful towards you

take some time to pause

breathe and invite God into the process.

Take time to see it for what it is

and release the energy from your spirit

take time to give it to your Higher Power

for healing and resolution.

Once you know....you can't not know.

When someone shows you who they are

believe them the first time.

Your only reaction should be

to smile and walk away.

MY THOUGHTS FOR THE DAY

Without loyalty and integrity to moral values

we are doomed to slither in the shadows

and continue reaping what we sew...

once our secrets hit the light of exposure

and we are able to stand in them and fully

embrace them for what they are...

that is when we will begin our journey

on the path to true enlightenment and change.

MY THOUGHTS FOR THE DAY

There are some human beings

that are vehicles of inspiration

they have a higher purpose in life

to spread the love in their hearts

with all who cross their path...

it is these souls whom I cherish the most

let's continue to shine

even during the darkest of times!

MY THOUGHTS FOR THE DAY

Each of us has a place in the world

a place where we shine bright

brighter than the sun

it's a God-given gift

that we alone must discover and make use of

we were born to shine....so let's do this

let's bask in the sunlight of the spirit

today is a new day

full of wonderful opportunities

to love one another and share our innermost selves with

there is no time like the present moment!

MY THOUGHTS FOR THE DAY

It is an extraordinary gift

to be able to bare your soul to another

and know they will cherish and honor your vulnerability.

MY THOUGHTS FOR THE DAY

We need to continuously move

in the direction of our goals

when we start getting close to the goal

morph it into something bigger

change it up so you always have

something to work and strive towards.

MY THOUGHTS FOR THE DAY

No matter what is happening around us

we have to make the journey magical.

MY THOUGHTS FOR THE DAY

When you give life all of your being

body, mind, and spirit

and it comes from an authentic place

the Universal gifts will be endless.....

MY THOUGHTS FOR THE DAY

Where does the song in your soul live?

What makes the melody burst with color?

Can I hear it?

Can I see it?

MY THOUGHTS FOR THE DAY

The soul exists

in beams of Light

let's shine!

MY THOUGHTS FOR THE DAY

When you come from

a pure, honest, vulnerable

place in yourself...

you touch that same place

in others.

MY THOUGHTS FOR THE DAY

Tell the truth no matter how much it hurts

you will grow from speaking your truth

and hopefully the receiver will too...

the truth will always set us free!

MY THOUGHTS FOR THE DAY

It is the breaking of a life

that produces the blessings of life!

The most blessed people on earth

are the ones that have gone through

something that has broken them down!

These blessed people are the warriors of the Light

they have a mission in their heart to share love and light

and nothing can stop them from SHINING!!!

MY THOUGHTS FOR THE DAY

MY THOUGHTS FOR THE DAY

Creativity

is a delicate flower

you must nourish it

and allow it to bloom

in its own time...

MY THOUGHTS FOR THE DAY

I would much rather be a tiny star

surrounded by other stars

striving for brilliance...

than a big fish in a little pond

full of people drowning

in their own mediocrity and stagnation!

Water seeks its own level....it's time to RISE UP!!!

MY THOUGHTS FOR THE DAY

Friendships....

It is survival of the fittest

some people lose oxygen

going up the mountain

they simply cannot

make the climb with you

they start dropping off

when the going gets tough

let them drop

the warriors of the light

will remain strong!

MY THOUGHTS FOR THE DAY

We are not defined

by what other people

say, think, or feel about us....

we are defined by the connection

we have with our Higher Power

and the feeling we get

while in the 'heart of God'....

MY THOUGHTS FOR THE DAY

The main lesson

of our trials and tribulations

is to bring us closer to the Source

of who we truly are

at our core....

MY THOUGHTS FOR THE DAY

We are bound to ideas of our own imagination and perception

whether they are positive or negative bindings

highly depends on the messages we received as a child

however as an adult we all have the power

to cleanse our perception with the sunlight of God's spirit

and re-write our story to be woven with beauty and greatness!

MY THOUGHTS FOR THE DAY

True friendship begins

when we can be vulnerable

with another human being

unafraid of exposing

our soul to their soul...

I am so grateful to the people

who make my heart

sparkle and shine!!!

MY THOUGHTS FOR THE DAY

God's purpose for our lives

dwells within our spirits

all we have to do

is quiet our minds enough

so that we can hear the messages

being laid upon us...

MY THOUGHTS FOR THE DAY

Spirituality can be explained

as our connection to God

and the awakening Divinity

of the human soul....

MY THOUGHTS FOR THE DAY

Spirituality is the cry of the soul

the longing to be intertwined

with the 'heart of God'

to be in the Light

to be one with the Great Beloved....

MY THOUGHTS FOR THE DAY

If you have an idea of who I am
or what you think I should be
without getting to know me first
then you are robbing yourself
of the amazing opportunity
to really know me
the real me
the woman who laughs and cries
and who expresses the way she feels
the woman who speaks her truth
the woman who loves with all of her being
when you judge me
through someone else's opinion of me
you energetically put up a wall between us
therefore cutting off any genuine friendship
we may have had...
it's time we all stop judging
and start loving more
life is short
before you know it
your life will be flashing before your eyes

make sure it is worth watching...

MY THOUGHTS FOR THE DAY

God understands our prayers

even if they are whispers from our Soul.....

MY THOUGHTS FOR THE DAY

Those with an inspired mind

sparkle and shine in the Light.....

MY THOUGHTS FOR THE DAY

Don't ever be afraid to fall in love

fall in love with as much as you can

the way your loved one's look at you

when you walk into a room

the sound of your best friend's laugh

the twinkle in your child's eyes

when you tell them how proud you are of them

the expression on your mom's face

when you tell her she is your hero

the feel of her hug

the smell of her skin

fall in love with life

with everything

it's waiting for you

it's time to Love

with every fiber of your being.....

MY THOUGHTS FOR THE DAY

When my mind is still

I am able to hear the messages

from my Soul with greater clarity.

When I am at one

with this pure Light energy

the Universe surrenders

for it knows we are One in the same.

MY THOUGHTS FOR THE DAY

All of my answers to life

have been found in my heart center....

that is where my greatest Love resides.

MY THOUGHTS FOR THE DAY

Our body-mind connection

is one that cannot be separated...

we cannot live a spiritual life

if we dishonor the body and vice versa.

The body affects our mental state

and our mind affects our physical state....

it is all One....all inter-related.

MY THOUGHTS FOR THE DAY

God dwells

within the deepest recesses

of your spirit

your heart

your soul

it is a never-ending supply

of peace and joy

we must go within the silence of our being

to connect deeply with this powerful Source

God is found within....not without

see you in the silence....see you in Love.....

MY THOUGHTS FOR THE DAY

9 781452 559711